MABEL

MABEL

Beyond the Round Black Box

SUELLEN M PALYA

MANY**SEASONS**PRESS

Mesa, Arizona • 2025

SECOND EDITION

MABEL, Beyond the Round Black Box

Copyright © 2025 Suellen M Palya

MANY**SEASONS**PRESS

Published by Many Seasons Press
an Imprint of Multimedia Publishing Project
123 N. Centennial Way, Suite 105
Mesa, Arizona 85201
480-939-9689 | MultimediaPublishingProject.com

Book designed by Yolie Hernandez
(AZBookDesigner@icloud.com)

Paperback ISBN: 978-1-956203-62-2

Library of Congress Control Number: 2024921574

Disclaimer: These personal events are shared in the interest of history. Names, places and dates are not exact. Personal feelings are only a matter of opinion. Take what you like and leave the rest. They are not intended to be judgmental or to create hostility or embarrassment. It is with a deep sense of loyalty and vulnerability that I share my feelings and with a deeper sense of respect that I mention friends and relatives who have touched my life. Thank you for being a part of my history; a part of my heart.

THIS BOOK IS DEDICATED TO the generations of children who were influenced by two women, Mabel Boehrs and Ava Schultz, who overcame, with courage, the health challenges presented to them.

Other Books by the Author

Mabel (First Edition)

Conversations With Kris:
Letters between a Mom and her Murdered Son

Spiritsong: One Woman's Journey

CONTENTS

PROLOGUE IX

SETTING THE SCENE XIII

Chapter 1 MEETING MABEL 1

Chapter 2 MOM GONE 5

Chapter 3 CARETAKERS 9

Chapter 4 OUR BACKYARD 17

Chapter 5 MOM'S RETURN 25

Chapter 6 SAYING GOODBYE 33

EPILOGUE 37

PROLOGUE

Memories

If I were to paint my memories

There would be no canvas large enough.

People, places and events parade through my thoughts,

A myriad of colors, rich texture and hue.

As my mind travels to the home of my girlhood

I move about the house as if I still lived there.

The grandfather clock sits in the same place of honor

Keeping time to the passing years

It watched me grow from child to teen.

I meander through the small town on gravel roads.

From one friend's house to another

I walk, the distance being short.

Five streets in any direction is the edge of town

I see cattails in ditches; hear the killdeer's warning sound.

Acres of flax and meadows of mustard,

The fields of my memory—how vast.

From "Glancing Back" 2009

SETTING THE SCENE

SETTING THE SCENE

TITLE: MABEL: BEYOND THE ROUND BLACK BOX

ACT I

Scene 1

(Cool, sunny morning in small kitchen of white clapboard farmhouse on North Dakota Prairie in 1940's. Twenty-five year old Mabel is helping her mother, Meta [first generation from Germany] make fresh bread dough for loaves and buns.)

MABEL: "There is a tuberculosis pandemic here in America. Our friends in Germany have already lost their lives to the contagious virus. I wonder if any neighbors in America will be affected."

META: (speaking with thick German brough) "Yah! It is sad they died so young."

(They stand in silence as they finish kneading the dough, setting it aside to rise and bake later in the large, black cast iron oven after adding another log to the fire box.)

(Later, with the smell of fresh bread filling the air, three visitors arrive at the farmstead to visit with Meta. Mabel hides in the shadows, feeling ashamed about the round, black box covering her right eye. She continues working in the kitchen to avoid being around people.)

Scene 2

(Cool, sunny morning in small North Dakota town of Crosby. George Schultz parks his Desoto near the back entrance to Crosby Electric Store he owns and repairs electrical equipment. With a large display of Maytag products in the front showroom, George works in the workshop on small appliances, specializing in small radios. He walks through the front showroom among refrigerators, washing machines and stove ranges to unlock the front door. With a coffee cup in his hand, he proceeds next door to check in with Chet Couee, the local barber. They spend coffee time talking about business in small town America before it gets too busy with locals needing services.)

Scene 3

(George's wife, Ava, is cleaning up breakfast dishes, washing them by hand. The three children are still sleeping and she starts making the daily bread in the small, narrow kitchen. Ava begins to feel a little weak and dizzy, her breathing making the work exhausting.

Two little girls come into the kitchen for Mommy hugs and cuddles before eating Corn Flakes cereal, while Mom waits for the bread dough to rise. Small brother Orbie John is still sleeping in his crib.

The two little girls leave the kitchen to get dressed to play outside. Ava grabs the kitchen counter as she feels another raspy cough rising from her lungs. Putting her handkerchief over her mouth she catches the mucus from the deep cough and sees a red blotch the size of a fifty cent piece on the white cloth. Feeling dizzy and sitting on a stool, she calls her husband, George, at work to ask for help.

After a short time George enters the back door, checks with Ava and goes to the phone to call Dr. McMoffit.)

ACT II

Scene 1

(Ava's sister, Bode, and her young daughter, Cleone, stand by the front door with Suellen, Linda, and little Orbie John, waving goodbye to Mom as she and Dad leave in the DeSoto toward San Haven, the Tuberculosis Sanitorium near Dunseith, North Dakota.)

Scene 2

(George and Ava share a conversation as they drive the two hour distance to the Sanitarium)

Scene 3

(George has mental dialogue with himself as he returns to Crosby. Who will care for the kids when I work? I've got to pay medical expenses now. I may have to take that job offer in Chicago for that high paying job training in Refrigeration. Dr. McPhail recommended Mrs B as a caretaker for the children. Could Ava's sister Bode help? I need to move from our small house to the larger home Doc Moffit has for sale on South Main. I can keep busy with a remodel. What will happen if I catch the tuberculosis from Ava?)

Scene 4

Childcare becomes a challenge until George contacts a family friend near the home farm in Donnybrook and Mabel comes to stay with his three children.)

Chapter 1

MEETING MABEL

WHEN I FIRST SAW MABEL, I hid behind my dad. I felt frightened of her, not because I was shy or she was someone I didn't know, but because she wore a round, black box over her right eye, held with an elastic strap around her hair. The black box, covered with black cotton material, was where her eye was supposed to be. She never allowed us to see what we could only imagine. It was scary to think that her eye was missing, or it was black and blue, red or white, or maybe green. I was only five years old at that time, with a vivid imagination, yet I only remember that Mabel was a beautiful person on the inside because that is what we saw as she cared for me, Suellen; my younger sister, Linda; and little brother, Orbie John.

Mabel spoke to me with her cheerful voice, "Come here, Suellen, and let me see how big you are. Your daddy told me about his three cute children. Here, I'll move over to make room so you can sit next to me."

Slowly and cautiously I moved closer to Mabel, with a little nudging from Dad, and soon found myself sitting next to her; studying her face up close. She had a fresh smell of soap about her as she reached out her thin, sun-tanned hand to gently touch my arm.

I was curious and asked, "Why do you cover your eye with that black box?"

Mabel answered matter-of-factly, "I hurt my eye!"

"How did you hurt your eye?" I inquired with sincere curiosity.

Mabel continued her story, "I fell from a horse when I was a little girl."

"How did the horse hurt your eye?" I continued as my dad watched protectively for Mabel's reaction.

"The horse stepped on this side of my face and I hurt my eye."

How do you sleep with that box over your eye?"

Mabel answered, "I lay on my other side."

Again I asked, "Did the horse really step on you?"

"Yes," was all she said. My curiosity was satisfied as we talked and I felt the warmth and comfort from her friendship. I felt reassured as she put her arm around my shoulders and gave me a slight squeeze. I wasn't feeling so frightened of her as she listened to my questions and answered with firm, non-threatening directness.

It was many years later we learned about the benign-growth behind her eye that started growing outward when she was in sixth grade. It was inoperable because of its nearness to many blood vessels. She changed the gauze dressing over her eye each day and custom fitted the black box to adjust to the growth of the tumor. Mabel would form a cardboard strip around the circumference of her eye; attach the ends and add a cardboard circle to enclose it.

She would cover the box with black cotton material and sew on an elastic strap to complete the task.

There were other big, round lumps on her cheeks, her forehead, her arms and legs. Her lips became crooked, pushed over by the box around her eye. Over the years a bag of flesh extended below the bottom of the black box. As it grew longer, Mabel wore a thin, silk scarf around her head to support the weight of the extra flesh.

At first, Mabel appeared scary and different. As time moved on, I grew to see Mabel as a beautiful, loving, caring human being without noticing the black box. One of her many gifts were the stories she told to satisfy our curiosity. She cuddled us with her sweet, firm voice and

encouraged us with positive reinforcement. She was kind and thought-
ful, a great listener, and always there.

Mabel made time to talk about our mom who was absent from
home for health reasons. She would comfort me with the hope of her
return to our family; she didn't know when, but reassured me when I
hoped it would be soon. We trusted that Mabel would be there when
we needed her. She would make mud pies with us and come for tea in
our playhouse. Life was good when I started school. Mabel braided my
hair in pigtails, found clean clothes and even had my long brown stock-
ings and garter belt clean and ready to wear. I hated those ugly, long,
brown socks and the garters that dug into my skin, but Mabel firmly
encouraged me to wear them.

My friends in the neighborhood learned to like Mabel too, and our
yard was filled with kids all the time. Mabel's homemade lemonade and
chocolate-chip cookies were a big draw, as well as her fairness and con-
sistent diplomacy with all of us. Mabel would say calmly, "Now, who had
the doll first? When Patty is finished playing with it, you can take your
turn to play with Betsy, the doll."

"But I want Betsy, now!"

"No! That's not fair. You need to take your turn. It's Patty's turn now.
It will be your turn next."

Mabel wiped our tears, cleaned bloody knees and held us close in
the rocker. She loved the dandelions we brought her and the pictures
we drew, too. It was a happy day when Mabel came to stay when Mom
was away in the hospital.

CHOCOLATE CHIP COOKIES

Preheat oven to 350 degrees. Get all the ingredients together. Crisco, white sugar, brown sugar, eggs, flour, baking soda, salt, vanilla, chocolate chips and walnuts. Measure 1 ½ cups Crisco into large mixing bowl. Measure and add ¾ cup white sugar and 1 ½ cups brown sugar. Mix with "beater" until white mixture is creamy smooth. Next add three eggs and watch as the mixture has a yellow tint. The flour comes next. First add 1 cup all-purpose flour along with 1 ½ teaspoon baking soda, 1 ½ teaspoon salt, and 1 ½ teaspoon vanilla. Add 2 ½ cups flour making it a total of 3 ½ cups flour. The extra half cup flour is the secret to a fine cookie. Use two small teaspoons to scoop the cookie mixture onto a cookie sheet. Four rows of three dough mounds make room for the cookies to expand. Each cookie sheet is left in the oven 10-12 minutes or until cookies appear light brown. Take out of oven, let cookie cool on cookie sheet for several minutes, then use baking spatula to remove from cookie sheet onto cooling rack. When cool, place in container and store in cool place. Yield: 4 dozen.

LEMONADE

Combine one cup sugar, one cup lemon juice and five cups water. Stir to dissolve sugar. Slice one lemon and add to lemonade. Serve over ice.

Chapter 2

MOM GONE

I WAS ONLY FIVE YEARS OLD when my mother, Ava, was diagnosed with active tuberculosis, the highly contagious respiratory illness requiring isolation and rest. The shades had been pulled over the sunlight of our family when she left for a year and a half to live in San Haven Tuberculosis Sanitarium in Dunseith, North Dakota. It was a traumatic time for our family. Dad was an electrician and owned an appliance business with a repair workshop in the back of his store in Crosby, North Dakota.

My dad, George Schultz, was a handsome, healthy, six-foot, young man of 30 when Mom became ill. He grew up on a farm in Donnybrook, North Dakota, a small rural community eighty-seven miles east of Crosby. He graduated from Kenmare High School where he lettered in football and other sports activities. After graduation, he attended Wahpeton State School of Science south of Fargo, North Dakota, gaining electrical skills. He worked for the John Iverson Company and bought an electric store from them in Crosby, North Dakota. He opened Crosby Electric Store in 1939.

Near his store was a bakery, "The Sweet Shoppe". My mom, Ava Doughty, worked there and Dad became a regular customer, sweet on Ava. Eloping to Plentywood, Montana, with Sam and Mabel Burner as witnesses, they were married by the Justice of the Peace on October 28, 1940. I arrived on December 9, 1941. While attending the movie "Gone

With the Wind" they decided to name their first-born daughter Suellen, who was a sister to Scarlett O'Hara in that movie.

Their first home was a small, two-bedroom bungalow on the North end of Crosby. They were blessed with three children: me, Suellen; my sister, Linda in 1943; and my brother, Orville (Orbie John) in 1945. A neighbor recalls seeing my mom each Saturday afternoon, taking a break from her three children, strolling uptown to meet friends for coffee. Mom would be dressed up in her finest suit, hat on head and red fingernails. She had beautiful hands with slim fingers and long fingernails. She was petite at five feet two inches.

In May of 1946 Mom was tragically diagnosed with active tuberculosis when blood appeared on her handkerchief after a coughing spell. Dr Moffit said it was time for "the rest", the only known treatment for the disease at the time. It meant being isolated from family and friends until the lungs could have a chance to heal. For some, the lungs never healed and death was imminent. The death toll from tuberculosis in 1946 was 91 in North Dakota and 50,911 in the USA.

The diagnosis of active tuberculosis meant the family was quarantined until the public health nurse completed a thorough assessment using the results of a Mantoux Skin Test, X-rays, and physical exam. Eventually, we were cleared to be among the public again. While quarantined we had to stay inside our home and I didn't understand why I couldn't play with my friends or why we couldn't go to the farm to see Grandpa and Grandma Schultz in Donnybrook. I felt excluded and different from my friends. I didn't feel as if I fit in, a devastating feeling that lasted through my adult years.

After Mom left for San Haven, we moved to a larger house on South Main Street in Crosby. There were lots of windows and an enormous staircase leading to two bedrooms and an attic upstairs. Dad had a big bedroom downstairs by the kitchen and dining room.

There was a large living room and an enclosed front porch on the house. A huge yard and an old lumbering, tall tree with wide branches for climbing was our outside playground.

While we played with friends, Mabel managed our household. I can recall Mabel washing and ironing clothes. She stood beside the narrow, wooden ironing board in the kitchen, the hub of activity, where she supervised the children outside the back screened door.

 With silent frustration, she adjusted the elastic strap holding the circular, black, cloth box over her right eye. On warm days she ironed and sweat was dripping from her face. She wore a headscarf over her wet, stringy, shoulder-length chestnut hair. She blinked her left eye to clear the dampness from her brow. The steam from the iron gives a freshly laundered odor from the white, cotton blouse she irons. Her body odor is less than fresh as she continues to sweat from her task of keeping clothing for the family of four in her care.

As she ironed, the children would run in from outside to go to the bathroom, show her salamanders they caught, or ask for a drink of water. Mabel would be able to carry on a conversation as she ironed or hung the clothes on a hanger before reaching for the next wrinkled item to be pressed.

Mabel started washing clothes in the cool morning hours. She carried the wet laundry outdoors in a wooden basket with wire handles to hang on the clothesline in the backyard. It is now early afternoon as she stands by the ironing board, carefully pressing the wrinkles from articles of clothing that had dried in the sun. The fresh ozone filled the air as she worked.

Dad's khaki work pants, dark-colored clothes and blue jeans still remain on the clothesline drying in the afternoon sun. Mabel's work on Wash Day filled many hours of her time. She would finish in time to prepare supper for the three children and their father. She had baked a hamburger macaroni hot dish which would easily be heated in the oven in time for the six o'clock meal. Glorified rice would be the salad for tonight with freshly-baked buns she made this morning while the first load of clothes were washing in the electric washer in the basement.

Mabel managed the household with skill and, I bet, she slept well after a full Wash Day.

HAMBURGER MACARONI HOT DISH

Brown diced onions in one Tablespoon butter in frying pan on the stove top. Add one pound hamburger. Brown and drain. Add one can tomato soup and one can tomato sauce. Simmer. Meanwhile, boil three cups water in five-quart saucepan. Add two cups elbow macaroni and dash of salt. Bring to boil; remove from heat, cover and let macaroni soak for ten minutes. Add hamburger mix to drained macaroni and bake in casserole dish at 350 degrees for 45 minutes.

GLORIFIED RICE

Bring two cups water to a boil and one cup white rice with dash of salt. Simmer for one hour and place in refrigerator to cool. Whip one cup cream. Add two Tablespoons sugar and one teaspoon vanilla, a small can of drained, crushed pineapple and whipped cream to cooled rice. Let sit in refrigerator to blend until ready to eat.

MABEL'S HOMEMADE BUNS

In a large mixing bowl, combine 2 cups flour and one package active dry yeast. In saucepan heat 1 cup milk, 1/3 cup sugar, 1 teaspoon salt, and 1/3 cup butter just until warm. Add to flour mixture. Add 2 eggs. Beat together. Stir in the remaining 2 or 2 ½ cups flour with a spoon. Turn onto floured surface making moderately stiff dough that is smooth and elastic. Shape into a ball. Place in greased bowl; turn once. Cover. Let rise in warm place. Punch down; divide dough in half. Cover and let rest 10 minutes. Shape into desired rolls and place on cookie sheet, Cover; let rise till nearly double in size. Bake at 375 degrees for 12 to 15 minutes or till golden.

Chapter 3

CARETAKERS

WHEN MON LEFT FOR SAN HAVEN, Dad knew he had to hire household help to care for us.

He was afraid of contacting tuberculosis from exposure to Mom's disease and was concerned about how he would manage to care for his three young children and continue to maintain a thriving electrical business with rural electricity just introduced to area farmlands.

"Old Mrs. B" was the first person that came to stay with us. She would sit in the rocking chair, twisting her fingers around and around each hand saying, "No, Suellen, get down from there. If you were supposed to have a cookie, you would have been given a cookie. And look at this one over there—Linda, who told you to wear your good shoes to go out and play? Suellen, take your sister upstairs immediately and find her play shoes. Well? What are you waiting for? Get going."

Grumpy "Old Mrs. B" would not come out to play when we asked her—Mom had. She would not come to see the mud pies we made when we asked her—Mom had. The gentle, soothing comfort of Mom was not there. I missed Mom's sweet smell when she held us close for comfort when we were hurt. "Old Mrs B" smelled like moth balls. I missed Mom's dancing, sparkling eyes when she saw our mud cakes laying on boards to bake in the sun and how we had decorated our mud pies with small, red honeysuckle berries and yellow cariganna blossoms. I missed Mom's delight to see how we arranged a tea party table with hollyhock "ladies," their upside-down blossoms for the skirt and an upright bud attached to the soft tip of the "skirt" for the head. The "lady" was flanked by a jagged elm leaf, which graced the table or floated on water for a centerpiece. I missed Mom's audience when we played house with real grown-up dresses, hats, gloves, and clunky old shoes that, to us, were new treasures. My favorite dress was long and lacy, flowing over the yellowed-white, open-toed high heels. The dress trailed behind as I clomp-clomped on the concrete sidewalk. My best friend, Nancy, wore a lavender straw hat with her frilly blouse and long, black skirt. Her pink, flat shoes flapped loudly as she strutted along. Patty, my neighbor from across the street, wore an orange, print dress with a white, fringed scarf over her curly black hair. Her brown suede heels click-clacked behind me.

"Let's have a parade," Patty's little sister, Vicky, shouted. The clamor and clank of many tin-can drums rang through the air with the gleeful shouts and giggles from all the kids in our neighborhood.

"Old Mrs B" yelled from the open screen door, "Quiet down out there!" Her straight, gray hair was drawn back in a bun and was covered with a hairnet, which pulled her face into a frown. She continued to wring her hands as if she were washing something away.

Mom had watched our parades and clapped her hands to the beat of the tin-can drums.

A lump of incredible sadness formed in my throat when I thought about Mom and how much I missed her.

"Old Mrs B" tried to take Mom's place cleaning, washing, ironing, and cooking meals. I didn't like the way she made me eat cottage cheese and I would gag to demonstrate my dislike when she told me to put a spoonful in my mouth. Tearfully and hesitantly I sat there until my plate was clean; the "Think of all the starving young children in China" comment never convinced me I should eat something so revolting to my taste buds and insulting to my throat as the curds backed-up traffic to my stomach.

The three of us kids had too much energy and caused too much trouble for "Old Mrs B".

She left our home shortly after she arrived, or so it seemed to me, for she wasn't with us long.

Aunt Bode and her nine-year old daughter, Cleone, came to care for us until another housekeeper could be found.

Aunt Bode was working for Dad as a secretary at the store. Cleone and Bode had just arrived from Minneapolis. Aunt Bode was a happy person who wore red lipstick and was Mom's sister. She was petite like Mom but much skinnier and fancy. She wore dresses all the time with skirts that swayed and twirled as she moved. She liked to wear high-heeled shoes and kept her fingernails painted red like Mom had. Aunt Bode was there with us, but it just wasn't the same. She was short and skinny, with bowed legs, her short, trim nails neatly painted a hot, red color. Her eyelids and lips were colored, too. Her voice was like the cooing of the mourning dove and her laughter and giggles would ring through the house when she was there during the day, but at night she was gone to movies or dances with her friends, Beulah and Rose.

I smelled sweet perfume as they walked out the door. I admired the sparkling, costume jewelry dangling from their ears. Skirts were swinging and swaying as they walked to Beulah's flashy, turquoise Chevy with the big, fancy fins. I could hear their sparkling laughter as the car pulled away. Breakfast was late on the mornings after a late night out. Aunt Bode seemed to drink many cups of coffee throughout the day and claim she had a headache.

She moved about very slowly, keeping busy with as little as possible. Lots of magazines got read on those days, but we also spent a lot of time with Grandpa and Grandma Doughty at their small, two-story house on the east side of town near the fairground. They were old and Grandma was in her downstairs bed all the time. Aunt Bode took care of them, too.

Grandpa would be my partner for a game of dominoes or checkers while Bode would cook and clean. While Grandpa napped, Cousin

Cleone and I played dolls in the dimly-lit, upstairs bedroom with the low, slanted ceiling.

"Come on!" I would say, "Let's jump up and down on the bed without hitting our heads."

It was a real challenge until Aunt Bode half-whispered through the floor grate, "You kids settle down! Grandpa is taking a nap!"

We got quiet once again until I said, "Let's put Linda on the mattress and bounce the bed with our hands." We giggled as Linda bounced up and down, up and down, her little head bobbing as we bounced her up and down. Her squeals of delight got louder and louder the higher she bounced.

Our giggles turned to laughter until we heard, "Get down here this instant!" Aunt Bode sent us outside where we found lots of mud puddles to play in, using sticks to make little ditches for the rainwater to move from one puddle to another. The afternoon would fly by before we returned home to get supper ready for Dad. Aunt Bode must have gotten tired with all the cooking, cleaning, and taking care of so many people.

My cousin, Cleone, became one of my best friends. Her four years seniority often left her to supervise the "little kids" while the adults were allowed to go into the Sanitarium to visit with Mom. When we traveled by car to San Haven, Cleone would be left "in charge" of us outside the huge, foreboding building where they kept my mom. The "San" appeared as big as the castle of the Mean Wicked Witch and I felt really scared as I searched each dark, ugly window for a glimpse of Mom. I imagined this forbidden castle swallowing my mom, never to be seen again. Chills climbed up my backbone and out over my skin. If I stayed there gawking, the horror seemed much too intense for this scared, little girl with the vivid imagination.

Pretending to turn the fears off like a light switch, I found myself running and shuddering with raging emotions as I cried out to my cousin up ahead, "Wait for me!"

We would play around the area by the pond where little frogs croaked and hopped from lily pad to lily pad as the sun danced on the water. There were goldfish to watch in the pond, green leaf-boats to float in the rippling water, and pebbles to skip over its smooth, mirror-like surface. Fascinating rings silently echoed across the pond as we counted each pebble jump.

Sometimes we played with our dolls, dressing and undressing them, each child taking a turn with the narration.

"You be the mom and I'll be the kid."

"No, I want to be the mom and you can be her sister."

"Okay, let's get dressed and go uptown for some coffee." The conversation continued, as the tree shadows lengthened.

During one particular visit, we were brought to an open window at ground level on the side of the towering, brick building. The window ledge was just my size and, squinting from the bright sunlight, I peered through the open window to see Mom far across the shady room, sitting in a chair, a blanket draped over her lap.

I reached out to kiss and hug her, but someone held me back, saying, "No, you cannot go near your mother. She is sick and is too weak to talk." Feeling confused and bewildered, I cried and reached out to my mom, only to be pulled away. Someone said, "Here! Your mom crocheted doll clothes for your dolls." Through my tears I saw a person inside the room hand me the doll clothes. They were wrapped in cellophane and the package felt cold in my hand. A chilly, empty wind moved in my heart. "We washed and sterilized them so your mother's germs cannot hurt you," the person said. Germs or no germs, I wanted to be right next to Mom. I wanted to feel her near me with the comfort of the strong love we had for each other.

Quickly, I removed the cold, smooth, crinkly cellophane and reached inside for the precious red and white dress. I hugged it to my chest and cried, "Mommy! Mommy!" I looked at Mom again and saw them push her away in her chair. "Why can't Mommy come home now?

Why can't Mommy talk to me? Why are they taking Mommy away, again?" I cried out. The unexplained emptiness returned to my little heart once more. As the sun fell low in the sky and the shadows got longer, our playtime came to an end as we returned home, without Mom.

Dad drove away slowly with Aunt Bode holding Orbie John between my sister and me in the back seat. Cousin Cleone sat up front with Dad as the sweet, heavy feeling of sleep enveloped each of us, calming the intensity of the emptiness of leaving Mom behind.

One day, when afternoon shadows were long, I came home from playing at Nancy's house. I felt hungry and thirsty and thought, "What's for supper tonight? I hope it is a macaroni and tomato hot dish with fresh white bread, spread with thick, creamy butter." I ran up the front steps, pushed the outside door open, ran through the sun room and pushed the door with many tiny windows and ran into silence. "I'm home," I called out.

No answer; only silence.

"Anybody home?" I ventured.

No answer; only silence.

I sat down on the bench by the empty table in the quiet dining room. I looked around the shadowy room; the only light was coming through the windows on the west, leaving square patches on the black shadows of the floor. It reminded me of a black and white checkerboard, only I didn't feel like playing. I felt very alone and it was scary with no one around. A lump filled my throat and seemed to put up a roadblock for my breathing. I sat staring at the checkerboard of light on the floor, silent tears starting to fill my eyes and run down my cheeks. Sobs started trembling, the roadblocks for my breathing pushed outward, and I cried out, "Someone! Come here!"

After crying and looking for an answer, I pushed a chair to the telephone on the hallway wall and called my dad at work. Between sobs I told him, I'm home alone," sniff-sniff, "and waiting for supper," sniff-sniff, "but everyone is gone," sniff-sniff.

"I'll come home right now," he said, sounding irritated for being interrupted at work.

"Where is Bode?"

"She's not here."

"Wait right there." The phone clicked and there was only silence, once again. I sat on the bench and waited for Dad to come home. Aunt Bode and the "little kids" arrived the same time as Dad. There were lots of sounds now. Orbie John was crying and Dad's gruff voice was asking Aunt Bode, "Where were you? Why isn't supper ready?"

Aunt Bode explained. "I lost track of time when I was shopping and visiting with people I ran into. It got later and later at the grocery store and I had to rush home to kids crying and you crabbing at me."

I got frightened as Dad's voice got louder and louder. "I hired you to be here when the kids need someone and to have meals on time. You are more interested in yourself than you are in the kids," he shouted angrily.

I trembled silently, watching and listening to the verbal battle around me. "Please, let it stop," I screamed in my head. I felt frightened when Dad yelled. His big, deep voice boomed and filled every room in our house.

"Fine!" Aunt Bode said. "You want supper? Fix it yourself. I'm not taking this anymore. Cleone and I are leaving and I won't be back." She swiveled on her new red high heels, her skirt billowed as she marched out the back door. She was crying a she slammed the screen door with a heavy bang.

The silence that followed was deafening. Our movements were slow as Dad said, "Take care of your brother, Suellen, while I figure out something to eat. Linda, here are your toys to play with until we eat." We had scrambled eggs for supper that night, soggy toast and milk.

Evening shadows were flooding the dining room and when Dad switched on the light, the shadows disappeared.

As Dad tucked us into bed that night I asked, "Who will be here if Aunt Bode doesn't come back?"

Dad replied, "I'll figure something out." The heavy load of emotional fatigue showed on his face. The deep creases of his forehead and the dark bags under his eyes told of the tremendous exhaustion he felt. I imagine he was overwhelmed with the responsibility of providing for his family and maintaining his work to support them.

Chapter 4

OUR BACKYARD

MABEL CAME TO STAY WITH US AFTER AUNT BODE LEFT. I had seen Mabel at family gatherings at the Donnybrook farm where we stayed when Dad traveled alone to visit Mom at the "San". Mabel lived five miles north of the Schultz family farm with her mom, Meta, her brother, Otto and his wife, Virginia. They would bring their three daughters, Janet, Carol, and Brenda. We would play in the farmyard while the adults visited or prepared the noon meal of fried farm chicken, mashed potatoes, apple salad with celery, walnuts and whipped cream.

There were jello salads, too, and fresh bread with homemade butter paddled from fresh churned cream. Fresh apple pie with homemade churned ice cream topped off the meal.

Janet had asthma like I did, so one time in the hayloft was out of the question as we both started coughing and wheezing. We found quiet ways to play with paper dolls or color books.

Brenda and Linda would explore other areas of the farmyard, running around playing tag or hide-and-seek.

We would go out to the barn to watch Uncle Orville, dad's brother, milk the cows.

Grandma would say, "You may go watch, but keep your dress and shoes clean." Uncle Orville sat on a three-sided wooden stool with a flat board nailed to the top. The cow seemed like a huge monster with its swishing tail.

"Stand back so Bessie doesn't swat you with her tail," Uncle Orville would say.

He made sure we didn't step into the manure ditch, too.

We stood back to see him wash the cow's milk sac and get a large, silver pail ready to catch the milk he squeezed from the sac. A big, orange cat came over to watch, too, when, all of a sudden, Uncle Orville aimed a stream of milk into the cat's face while the cat licked at the milk and then cleaned its face with her paws. It would make us giggle to see the show.

Our backyard in Crosby was full of adventures, too.

"Push me! Push me, next! No! Push me!" rang the children's voices, taking turns on the swing by the side of our house. I loved to swing and hear the c-r-e-e-e-a-k of the rope around the tree limb or the sharp clank of the metal chain at the playground. The swing was like a magnet as I couldn't walk by without being swept off my feet with a fling in the swing.

We were just kids. Our neighborhood was our world, living on the south end of the "main drag" of Crosby. It was here I would escape from the lonely, empty world without my mom, whose absence from our home created within me an overwhelming crisis for such a little kid of six years old. Playing outside was all I could do to escape the ache of missing her so much.

Each day I would ask Mabel, "When is Mom coming home?"

Mabel, wise and compassionate, answered, "Someday. I know you miss her so much.

Now, go find your friends and play. I'll make chocolate chip cookies and lemonade, later." I trotted off, somewhat reassured, my need for security once more affirmed. I found my friends near the playhouse in my backyard.

My dad purchased the structure from some farmer where he had installed the wiring for REA (Rural Electric Administration). I was as excited as a farm family with electricity when he brought it home and put it behind our house. It was a one-room wooden playhouse, just tall enough for kids. It had a front porch on the west, a window opening to the north and another to the south where shouts radiated into the neighborhood; sometimes angry, sometimes sweet and sometimes daring. Secrets were shared about friendships, sisters and brothers. Anyone who repeated what was said was no longer considered a friend, which usually lasted for no more than a day.

Our playhouse provided a necessary sanctuary for my imagination, an escape from the emotional chaos of the "real world." The playhouse transformed from a family home to a school classroom; a candy store, bakery, or grocery store. In winter, there was good sledding from its rooftop to the ground after a blizzard would pile snowdrifts that covered the windows on the sides.

It was the hiding spot for hide-and-seek games or the middle obstacle for "Ante-I-Over", a catch-the-rubber-ball game. It was so much fun to catch the ball and run to the other side of the playhouse, quickly tagging someone from the opposing team. The screams were deafening as Vicky tried to run away, but was tagged and taken back to our side.

Often, the many girls and boys in our neighborhood would gather in the large empty lot between our home and our neighbors to the north. "Red Rover, Red Rover send Linda right over." Off Linda would run toward our side as her team jumped and shouted, "You can make it, Linda. Run! Run!" She dodged all the players from our team and reached our side without being tagged. Her prize was taking Nancy from our team to join the other side. Their team won because it had the most people when lunchtime rolled around.

The backyard provided a safe place to gather with friends to fill the empty space left by Mom. Some days this large space was "just the right size" for an intimate game of croquet, the clunk of the wooden mallet finding its target on the red, yellow, green or blue-striped wooden ball.

The sound echoed in the smoky afternoon air of autumn as it raced toward the silver, wire-hoop goal with enough force to enter the hoop and roll through. That feat earned another turn in the race to the two-foot wooden stake, which signaled the winner of yet another challenge. It was especially sweet when I could win the game with Jerry, the cute "boy next door." He was the "boy of my dreams."

Dreams invaded my alone time. Cutting out paper dolls became my passion as I pretended that it was me who had all the pretty clothes. Changing from one outfit to another made my monologue seem like a dialogue: "Okay, Betsy, let's try on your long dress for the dance tonight. Sandra, you put your long dress on, too, and we'll be models."

"Okay," Sandra said. "We'll be the prettiest girls at the dance."

Betsy continued, "All the boys will dance with us and swing us around the dance floor."

"I hope I don't trip and fall on my face which is so-o-o-o embarrassing," Sandra cried.

"Gee, Sandra, do you think Mom and Dad will chaperone the dance and see how much fun we are having?" Betsy asked.

"I don't know if Mom will feel good and Dad won't go by himself, you know," Sandra added."

"Gee, you're right," Betsy agreed. Sad, depressed feelings started creeping in—too close for comfort. It was a pattern and signaled that it was time to cut out more paper doll clothes and push sad thoughts out. No wonder I had two bureau drawers full of paper dolls.

"Let's go play tennis, Betsy." The mono-dialogue began again.

"Okay, Sandra," Betsy said with glee. "Let's wear pedal pushers, saddle shoes, and a shirt."

Sandra asked, "Are the boys going to be there, too? They always laugh at us when we miss the ball. I hope they stay away 'cause they only cause trouble."

By the end of two hours or more, I had been to the tennis court, the swimming pool, and the dance, in my dreams, alone in my room. There was time to color, cut and paste before lunch. Then it would be time to go outside and play with my real friends.

We spent a lot of time together, that neighborhood "gang of mine". On "dress up" days we played happy families. "I'm the mom and you are the dad, Greg. Patty and Vicky are our kids. No one is gone and we can go shopping together," I dictated. We always had lots of money to spend, bought whatever we wanted to eat and were so happy.

The girls always wore clothes that reached the ground. They accessorized with hats, gloves and purses. The boys wore big shirts, ties, and felt, derby hats. We could be seen tromping to the store, to church, or to the park for a picnic.

One sunny afternoon it was time for tea on the front porch of the playhouse where Linda, Nancy and I sat waiting for our tea party to begin. We were dressed in our grown-up clothes, pretending to be the "hoity-toity" ladies of an exclusive neighborhood, gathering to share secrets, gossip and experiences over "lemonade tea" and warm, delicious chocolate chip cookies.

The afternoon tree shadows were beginning to form when Mabel left the kitchen of the "big house" with a plate of freshly baked chocolate chip cookies in one hand and a pitcher of lemonade in the other. She moved down the gray, wooden steps into the backyard and glided toward the porch of the playhouse.

"Here comes our servant, now," I announced to the small group as Mable approached.

"Here you are Madame," Mabel played along, affirming me. Her presence helped me to feel no different from my friends whose mothers were home taking care of them and not staying far away in a hospital.

"You may place the plate of cookies here and pour tea," I instructed.

Mabel obliged with, "Yes, Madame."

"Do you think the sun will shine all day?" Linda questioned.

"I do hope so," Nancy replied. "My laundry smells so fresh and clean and is so crisp when it dries outdoors on the clothesline."

"Ironing clothes is absolutely boring for me. I'm so glad Mabel does the work," I added.

We seemed to be in a different world—a different time where all about us was lovely.

Our neighbors from across the street interrupted our reveries. Greg, Patty and Vicky, came with a round, blue rubber ball asking, "Wanna play Ante-I-Over?" The aroma of fresh chocolate chip cookies had called to them across the street and they got their share as the "hoity-toity" ladies shed their fancy dresses to choose sides for another favorite game.

My side won, in my mind of course, by truth or default because of the strong need to be a "winner" when "losing" was a real issue in the ever-encompassing "real world". The need for perfection was the drive to survive the chaos of "losing my mom at such an early age. Being bossy became the pattern of my behavior to feel the power of control in the uncontrollable events of Mom being gone from my real world. When friends left me out of activities, I felt devastated and ashamed that my mom was gone and their mom was home. Verbal spats seemed absolutely deadly.

"You can't come over to my house because Nancy doesn't want to play with you," Patty quipped. "You are too bossy and you always need to win."

Back to my paper dolls I shuffled where I found many play friends who would bring a semblance of order to my solitude. Even Mabel knew I needed to be alone with my "fantasy friends" for a short time where the frightened little girl inside me once again felt safe and secure. It was reassuring to know Mabel was there and was always my friend.

"Let the kids play together now and later they will come around again to ask you to come out and play," instructed Mabel in her matter-of-fact voice.

So it was that paper doll, Betsy, arranged for paper doll, Sandra, to come along to play on the pretend beach in our backyard. After lunch, Patty was at the back door asking Mabel, "Can Sue come out and play"

Eagerly I ran past Mabel saying, "Want to go swing?"

"Sure," Patty answered shyly. I was glad to be her friend again and knew Mabel was a kind, wise friend, too.

The last lazy days of late summer announced the beginning of my first year in school.

There were lots of my neighborhood friends starting school together. Gone were the mudcakes, the tin can parades, and the playhouse tea parties. Red Rover, Red Rover, games with jacks and a small rubber ball, and metal swings on the school playground took their place.

Mom was still gone, too. Mabel took particular care to make sure my hair was braided and my clothes were clean for that first day of school. She took a picture of me so Mom could see I was ready for school.

FRIED FARM CHICKEN

One whole fryer cut up in pieces. Heat 3 Tablespoons butter and 3 Tablespoons Crisco in a cast iron frying pan. Dip each piece of chicken in mixture of 2 cups flour, 1 teaspoon salt, 1 teaspoon pepper, and 1 teaspoon paprika. Fry until golden brown; remove from fry pan, place in 9" by 13" shallow baking dish and bake one hour in oven at 350 degrees.

APPLE SALAD

Cut four red apples into cubes. Soak in salt water to prevent browning. Drain. Toss with sliced celery and walnuts. Add whipped cream and serve chilled.

CHERRY JELLO SALAD

Boil two cups water. Add one package cherry jello. Stir to dissolve. Add 1 cup cold water and 2 cups ice cubes until jello becomes thick. Remove any remaining ice cubes. Let sit in refrigerator until wobbly. Cover with whipped cream and serve.

APPLE PIE

Peel and slice six, red apples. Soak in salt water to prevent browning. Drain. Add 1 cup white sugar, 2 Tablespoons flour, ½ teaspoon ground cinnamon, dash ground nutmeg, and 1 teaspoon grated lemon peel. Pour into uncooked pie crust. Add slices of butter, cover with another uncooked pie crust, crimp edges, sprinkle crust with cinnamon and sugar. Bake at 375 degrees for 50 minutes.

Chapter 5

MOM'S RETURN

THERE WAS A TWINKLE IN HIS EYES as he began to whistle while driving to visit Mom at San Haven. I didn't remember Dad whistling like this. I caught the twinkle when he took his eyes off the road, looked into the rear view mirror, and listened to the tune he whistled. It was then he started singing the words, with his rich baritone voice coaxing me to sing along.

"Cruisein' down the river on a Sunday afternoon…" It was a Sunday in May and we were cruisein' down the highway in a '45 Ford. Mabel was riding in the front seat with Dad. I sat behind the driver and Linda sat by the opposite window. Orbie John was between us.

"The birds above all sing of love, a gentle sweet refrain…," Dad sang as the car entered the Turtle Mountains, a contrast from the flat prairie we left behind. There were more trees here and I imagined birds of all kinds, sitting on the branches, chirping along with the song we sang.

I loved to listen to Dad sing. His singing voice was full and sweet, quite a contrast from the gruff speaking tone he most often used after a long day at work. The sound was comforting as it lilted about us as if to say everything was all right and that was something I longed to hear more often. Fears no longer existed when I sang with my dad.

"Maresey Doats and Doesey Doats and little Lambsey Divy…" Its whimsical melody made this tune sound like nonsense syllables as Dad

25

drove along. Sometimes my tongue got in the way and twisted in and around as I tried to sing along. Giggles wiggled their way out as the words tickled the roof of my mouth.

"Stop singing, Daddy. I can't get the words right."

Dad stopped and said slowly, "Mares eat oats." I repeated the words and listened to the next phrase, "Does eat oats." Again I repeated it hesitantly.

Dad sang slowly and deliberately, "Mare eat oats and does eat oats...", while I sang along. I enjoyed this time, singing with Dad. We shared a love of music since I was three years old. At that time, I was allowed to put big, round 78's on the phonograph. I would dance around, sing and clap while relishing the attention from both Mom and Dad. That was before Mom got sick.

It was my turn to sing along, and slowly I began, "Mares eat oats and does eat oats and little lambs eat ivy." To me it sounded like, "Mareseydoats and Doeseydoats and Little Amseydivy. It was many years later the words by rote took on meaning about mare, does and little lambs. All that really mattered was Dad's undivided attention. It made a long trip seem shorter and my empty heart a little fuller. Soon, unknown to me, something would happen to fill my heart with overflowing joy.

"I'm going to buy a paper doll that I can call my own..." Dad sang. It was his favorite song with a melody that climbed up and back down again. I loved this song, too, and moved my head from side to side as my French braids tapped a steady rhythm on each ear. Mabel usually braided my fine, whispy hair. The narrow end of the braid was brought up and attached with a bow or barrette to the wide strands at the beginning of the braid. I'd get mixed up and say 'barnet' instead of barrette.

Mabel had taken extra time to braid our hair before we left. Orbie Johns blond strands were parted on the side and slicked over the top of his head. All of us wore brand new, white leather, tie-shoes over clean white, cuffed, socks. Orbie John had pale yellow shorts with suspenders over a crisp, cotton, short-sleeved shirt. My sister, Linda, and I each wore pleated gabardine skirts with suspenders over the crisp, cotton, short-sleeved blouses Mabel had pressed so carefully. Linda's skirt was red and my skirt was navy blue. Standing together, we appeared to announce an important patriotic event.

An important event was about to happen as the shiny car wound its way along the curves, gently climbing toward San Haven. The large, four-story brick building shone in the noon-day sun as each window gleamed it's welcome greeting, a stark contrast to the foreboding shadows of previous visits. We were singing, "…K-K-K-Katie, beautiful Katie, I'll be waiting by the k-k-k-kitchen door," as we turned into the driveway leading to the front entrance of the "San".

I suddenly stopped singing as I recognized one of the three people sitting on white wooden lawn chairs. As the car approached, two of the people, who were dressed in white, starched nurse uniforms, stood up and walked over to the one person who remained seated. I saw Mom gently wave, dabbing her eyes with a white, cotton, embroidered hanky.

Dad stopped the car, turned off the engine, and opened his door. I saw a silvery stream drop from each of his eyes as he turned to shut the car door. He walked up to Mom, took both her tiny, pale, narrow hands in his large, tanned, wide hands and gently embraced her as she stood to greet him. They looked at each other, for what seemed a long time to me, before walking toward the car.

Mabel was waving as they approached the car. As she turned around to say, "Here comes Mommy," I saw the same silvery stream fall from one eye on Mabel's face. It looked like the same silvery streams running down Dad's face.

"Was Mommy coming to the car for a visit?" I wondered, trying to figure out what what was happening. Mom had never walked so close to them. Now Dad was opening the back car door where Linda sat and took her hand to help her get out of the car. Mommy put her arms around Linda for a hug as Linda hugged her skirt. Daddy reached in for

Orbie John and lifted him out for Mommy to hug. Orbie John looked at Mommy as he quickly placed a small kiss on her cheek.

Now it was my turn to move toward the open door to greet Mom. I waited hesitantly for a cue to reach out to Mom, afraid someone would tell me I could not touch her because she was sick.

"Come here, Sue, I have lots of hugs for you. We need to catch up. I've missed you so much and I've been saving all these hugs for you." I bounced across the back seat on cue and reached my arms out toward Mom.

"Oh, Mommy! I've been saving hugs and kisses for you, too. I love you, Mommy."

It felt safe to feel close to Mom again. I glanced over at the outdoor car mirror and saw the silvery streams on my face, too. Mommy held me close and stroked my braids.

"Mabel has taken good care of you kids. Look how nice you look. It reminds me of an American flag when you all stand together. We all have our freedom again. The doctor said I can go home with you today."

"Really, Mommy? Really? Really?" I twirled around as my skirt whirled and my heart swirled with joy and happiness. "Mommy's coming ho-ome! Mommy's coming ho-ome!," I sang in my very best sing-song voice. "The birds will sing that it is Spring and Mommy's coming ho-ome."

Mommy giggled and clapped. "Listen to my little songbird. Where did you learn to sing like that?"

"From Daddy! We sing a lot of songs together."

"Well, come on my little nightingale. We'll go say goodbye to the goldfish in the pond while Daddy loads the car."

With Mabel, Linda, and little Orbie John trailing behind, I walked with Mom, hand-in-hand under the soft umbrella of shade from the tall trees surrounding the lily pond.

"Bye, little froggy. Bye, little fly. Bye, Goldfish. It's time to say good-bye," I sang as I skipped around the pond, waving my hand and throwing little kisses at Mommy, then circled once again. I stopped to hug Mom and kiss her on the cheek. "I'm so glad you are all better, Mommy."

"I will still need lots of rest when we get home. I need to take lots of naps." We made our way slowly back to the car and Daddy helped Mommy get into the front seat while Mabel ushered me into the back seat first, then scooted in with Orbie John on her lap, while making room for Linda to get settled in as Daddy closed the car door and made his way over to the driver's place. As the car motored its way from the "San" toward home in Crosby, Daddy was singing, "Cruisein' down the river on a Sunday afternoon…" I opened my mouth to sing along but found only a wide, deep yawn as my braids pushed my sleepy head toward Mabel's shoulder. The peaceful waves of exhaustion cruised me down the river of blissful sleep until we arrived home, this time with Mom.

It was the beginning of life again with Mom at home. Mabel celebrated her return and stayed, not only to help with the laundry, cleaning, and cooking, but to serve as a caretaker for Mom, as well. They worked together, talking about the routine of everyday life and planning meals. Mabel still washed clothes, hung them on the outdoor clothesline, and ironed in the kitchen to keep an eye on us kids.

She still made chocolate chip cookies, fresh lemonade and brought it outside on a tray for all of us. Cornbread with homemade hot maple syrup became a favorite food at mealtime.

It meant a celebration, sitting around the table as a family, giving thanks that Mom was, once again, a part of the gathering. Sometimes, it was cornbread for Sunday brunch or cornbread for a rainy day lunch. It was great for supper, too.

Each meal always began with prayer and the Amen signaled it was time to eat. After Dad took the first piece from the middle of the baking dish, I "dibbed" for one of the taller, fluffy middle pieces. I sliced the top from my piece of steaming hot cornbread, flipped it over and spread the soft, creamy, rich butter over both sides. Hot homemade maple syrup over the top completed the ceremony and I was ready to enjoy the warm, grainy texture on my tongue as I inhaled the rich, sweet aroma of maple. The other kids chose pieces around the outside and, as before, Mom waited until everyone was served and only then, chose the piece of cornbread that was left in the baking dish.

My mom, Ava, was so grateful to be at home with her family. She had gotten stronger after a year and a half in the "San", but Doc McPhail felt she needed more rest to stay strong.

Much as she hated to admit it, he was right. She felt stronger as she sat with her family for this meal, scanning around the entire table to observe unique actions of each person and thanking God for the strength she was given to return home.

Dad often said, "Be real quiet; your mom needs her rest so she won't get sick." As the oldest, I thought I knew what that meant: *"You set a good example for the little kids. Don't whine or act crabby because you will make your mom sick and she'll have to leave home."* That was the worst thing that could happen: Mom getting sick and leaving home again. So it was, I disregarded my needs and stuffed my feelings. I was not going to make Mom sick again.

It became my mantra: "We need to play outside 'cause Mom is resting; Mom has to see the doctor today; she needs her pneumo shot; the nurse is coming this afternoon for our check-ups; this patch sure is itchy; is the public health nurse coming today?" The language of health became an everyday topic among conversations spoken or heard and the guarding of Mom's health remained an underlying concern. Yet, life continued to happen and events around growing children were predictable: patching up skinned knees, comforting friendship disputes, and chasing away boredom. Each day was a stepping stone for me, toward a semblance of order and a sense of security moment by moment with Mom still at home.

Girl scouting offered me the opportunity to participate in Community events. My brownie troop marched in parades; we had bake sales and went to Day Camp where I learned many skills. I especially liked the arts and crafts and was proud when I could start a fire. Crafts created treasures I kept for a lifetime. For Scout sleepovers, Mom made me soft, cozy, flannel pajamas. I found a note Mom had written in the pocket saying, "Have a good time. I love you. Mom."

Life was good for a young girl approaching her teen years, and especially good with Mom at home once again.

CORNBREAD

Sift together 1 cup yellow corn meal, 1½ cup all-purpose flour, ¼ cup white sugar, 4 teaspoons baking powder and ½ teaspoon salt in small mixing bowl. Make a hollow area in the middle of the dry ingredients and pour in 1 egg, 1 cup milk, and ¼ cup melted butter which have been stirred together. Beat with rotary beater until smooth; about one minute. Bake in greased 8" square baking dish in pre-heated oven of 400 degrees for 20 to 25 minutes. Cut into nine pieces and serve immediately.

HOT MAPLE SYRUP

Put 2 cups white sugar in medium saucepan. Pour 1 cup boiling water into sugar. Dissolve sugar and place saucepan over heat to bring mixture to a full rolling boil. Remove from heat and add 1 teaspoon maple flavoring. Can be served immediately. Stores well in refrigerator.

CHOKECHERRY SYRUP

Boil 3 ½ cups chokecherry juice. Add 5 cups sugar. Bring to boil for 2 minutes. Use on potato pancakes, crepes, cornbread, waffles or homemade buttered bread.

To make jelly, boil 3 ½ cups chokecherry juice. Add 1 package Sure Jell and ½ teaspoon butter (to keep it from boiling over). Bring to boil, stirring all the time. When it is a full rolling boil, add 5 cups of sugar. Bring to boil for 2 minutes and put in jars and seal.

Chapter 6

SAYING GOODBYE

MABEL STAYED IN OUR HOME FOR ONE MORE YEAR. She left for long weekends at her home near Donnybrook to visit her family. The day came when Mabel returned to the farm to live with her family. Mabel sat down beside us and explained that Mom was getting stronger and was able to cook and wash clothes again. A new washer and dryer made doing the laundry easier for her: Dad bought her a Mangler and later an Ironright where Mom could sit and iron clothes on a big roller. Mabel saw her get stronger each day.

Mabel told us we would always be her family because she loved us very much. A silver stream appeared on the left side of her face as she said goodbye. We were sad to see her go.

We walked her to the car and her brother, Otto, took her suitcase and placed it in the trunk. We hugged Mabel goodbye and waved until we couldn't see the car after it turned the corner. Mom was there to hold our hands and tell us that Mabel was a good person who helped us a lot, but it was time for her to be back at her family's farm.

Later, Mabel and her mother, Meta, moved to a small home in northwest Minot when I was a Junior in high school. We visited Mabel and Meta in their home and they would come to our home and make lefse, a Norwegian potato bread flattened into circles and browned on a round, hot grill. We spread fresh, creamy butter on the lefsa and sprinkled sugar before we rolled it up. It was a great treat.

We stayed in touch with Mabel. On the Fourth of July we would all meet on the Mattei farm by Donnybrook. Mabel was always glad to see us and admire how we had grown. All the ladies brought good food and after serving the meal we all sat in a circle of lawn chairs to visit. The ladies watched the game of softball we played on the lawn until the sun set. It was time to light fireworks, the end of a good time together.

The car headlights flooded the lawn as we gathered our clean dishes from the kitchen, that last cookie, and crawled into the back seat of the car where sleep came quickly from all the fresh air, sunshine, and exercise.

We visited Mabel and Meta in Minot. Mabel was caring for a six-year-old girl, whose Mom was a pilot flying her airplane in the Powder Puff Derby. We all played together in Mabel's home on a nice summer day. We had to be careful the screen doors were closed so Mabel.s pet parakeets wouldn't fly away. Mabel let them fly inside the house and when she served tea and cookies, she put them in their home for a nap. She covered the cage with a towel so the birds would think it was nighttime when their whistles and chirps would stop. Mabel was wearing a headscarf all the time as the flesh grew below her large, black box. Soon it was the end for both Mom and Mabel.

Mom, Ava, died in 1973, shortly before Mabel. Mom died from heart arrest due to complications from tuberculosis. Mabel and Meta attended her funeral.

The day arrived when Mabel was in bed all the time—still with her scarf over the bag of flesh below the large, circular black box. She died in her sleep and her mother, Meta, said she went peacefully. Mabel left a legacy of love and unconditional acceptance.

Their work on earth was done. They no longer had health challenges and the choir of angels increased by two.

LEFSE

Peel and boil enough red potatoes (5 lbs) to make 8 cups mashed potatoes. Mix 8 cups mashed potatoes with ½ cup heavy cream, 8 Tablespoons butter, 2 teaspoons salt, and 4 teaspoons sugar. After cooked, add 3 cups flour and roll out rounds of dough on pastry cloth, paper-thin. Bake on lefse grill until lightly browned on both sides. Turn with long lefse stick. Move baked lefse to cotton dish towel. Stack lefse and cover with cotton dish towel overnight. Pack in plastic bags the next morning. Spread lefse with butter, sprinkled sugar, roll up and eat.

Mabel and her two grave markers.

EPILOGUE

MABEL AND MOM AVA have definitely enriched my life with their presence. I am filled with gratitude for their gifts of patience, compassion and dignity. Mabel's legacy formed my relationship with myself and others through the lessons I learned from sharing, from time to process my great loss, and from her constant care and presence. Mabel's legacy renewed my hope in Mom's recovery from her illness, from her return home, and Mom's patience with challenges that came her way.

In the years that followed, my teaching career allowed me to show compassion towards my students, express patience in the learning process and joy in the achievements each of them created. In my counseling career, I understood loss, grief and reconciliation. I gained courage to face my responsibilities with dignity and forgiveness. My life is rich and full of friends, children, grandchildren and great grandchildren. It is my hope that sharing my story gives you, the reader, courage to recognize the strength it takes to face challenges as they arrive with hope and dignity. You don't have to do it alone.

The recipes I included are foods that provided a sense of comfort and safety during those early years. Eventually I learned to recognize the emotional buttons of loneliness, exhaustion and companionship that led to eating to fill the empty heart when Mom was away from home.

Live with peace and purpose, dear reader.

www.ingramcontent.com/pod-product-compliance
Lightning Source LLC
Chambersburg PA
CBHW041630140626

46547CB00031B/1954